AN ALPHABET
OF OLD FRIENDS

—— and ——

THE
·ABSURD·
A·B·C

AN ALPHABET OF OLD FRIENDS

——— and ———

THE ·ABSURD· A·B·C

by Walter Crane

The Metropolitan Museum of Art
and Thames and Hudson
New York

This volume is reproduced from "An Alphabet of Old Friends," published in *Goody Two Shoes' Picture Book*, and *The Absurd ABC*, both in the collection of The Metropolitan Museum of Art, gifts of Mr. and Mrs. Bryan Holme.

Published in 1981 by The Metropolitan Museum of Art and Thames and Hudson, New York.
© 1981 The Metropolitan Museum of Art

Library of Congress Cataloging in Publication Data:

Crane, Walter, 1845-1915.
 An alphabet of old friends; and, The absurd ABC.

 An alphabet of old friends originally published 1874; The absurd ABC originally published 1874.
 Summary: In the first of these two volumes, the letters of the alphabet are presented through illustrated traditional nursery rhymes and in the second, they are introduced with humorous illustrations and verses.
 1. Alphabet rhymes. 2. Nursery rhymes. 3. Children's poetry. [1. Alphabet. 2. Nursery rhymes] I. Crane, Walter, 1845-1915. Absurd ABC. 1981. II. Title.
PZ8.3.C85A1 1981 398'.8 [E] 81-9449 AACR2
ISBN 0-87099-272-4 (Metropolitan Museum)
ISBN 0-500-01260-1 (Thames and Hudson)

Produced at The Metropolitan Museum of Art by the Department of Special Publications. Printed and bound in Japan.

Preface

It is hard to imagine a time when there were no children's books at all, let alone books illustrated in color. But before the beginning of the last century there were virtually none. Even after the invention of the powered printing press in 1810, it was twenty years before the earliest, crudely printed, mass-produced color books began to appear on publishers' lists. It was at least another thirty years before fine engraving and printing, as we know them today, became possible and could be used to produce popularly priced children's books.

The pioneer in this field was Edmund Evans, who aside from being the best color printer in London, combined instinctive good taste with a shrewd business sense. Evans was always in search of new talent to design books that would both enhance his image and help keep his press at Racquet Court busy at slack times. One of the earliest, and quite the most profitable, of Evans's discoveries was Walter Crane.

Not only was Crane, then an unknown twenty-year-old artist, soon to start earning for himself the reputation he has today as "father of the illustrated children's book" and "archduke of the nursery," but he was also to become one of the most prolific artist-illustrators of his or any other day. Crane's talents were by no means confined to illustration. He became a noted designer of ceramics, stained glass, textiles, and wallpaper, as well as one of the most popular painters of the Pre-Raphaelite school. His painting *The Lady of Shalott* was accepted by London's Royal Academy when he was only seventeen years old; many of his masterpieces—including *Neptune's Horses* and *The Dance of the Five Senses*—hang in European museums.

Walter Crane was born in Liverpool on August 15, 1845, but within a few months his family moved to Torquay, in Devonshire. His father, an artist of considerable repute, was a strong influence on Walter, who at the age of six already displayed an exceptional talent for drawing. The boy's general schooling appears to have been fragmentary and certainly always took second place to his interest in drawing and painting. At the age of thirteen, after his family had left Torquay to live in London, Walter apprenticed himself to an engraver named William James Linton. No better training ground for an illustrator could possibly have been chosen, and after three profitable years with Linton, a confident young Crane tucked a few sketches under his arm and set out to comb the London publishing world for free-lance work. He was never long without an assignment, mostly hack work, but it remained for him to find his lucky star in the form of the enterprising printer Edmund Evans.

At first, Crane illustrated anonymously an unknown number of so-called "Mustard Plaster" or "Yellow Back" children's books, which were of commercial but little artistic merit. Within a year, however, Crane came into his own with his first three quality "Toy Books": *The House That Jack Built*, *Dame Trot and Her Comical Cat*, and *The Affecting Story of Jenny Wren*, all printed by Edmund Evans in 1865.

That children's books could now be so well illustrated, so beautifully printed in color, and sell for a very modest sixpence delighted the Victorian parent to such an extent that the bookshop became a regular port of call, and one of the biggest booms in publishing history was under way.

Following his first three successes in 1865, Crane continued to design an average of three books a year for the next ten years. While some of his earliest "Toy Books" were published by Frederick Warne & Co., certainly after 1866 all of his "Toys" appeared under the George Routledge & Sons imprint, either in their "Aunt Mavor Series" (later known as the "Sixpenny Toy Series") or in their shilling series, "Walter Crane's Toy Books."

In all of these, Crane brought a new high standard to illustrated children's books and remained unchallenged in the field until Randolph Caldecott and Kate Greenaway, both discovered by Edmund Evans, entered the competition in the late 1870s. The famous trio then became the top best sellers and remained so for many years to come. Caldecott died in 1886 when he was only forty years old; Greenaway lived until 1901, the year Queen Victoria died; and Crane lived on until 1915.

The subjects of Crane's books alternated between nursery rhymes, such as *Sing a Song of Sixpence* (1866) and *This Little Pig Went to Market* (1870), and classic fairy tales, which were brought back into favor in the Victorian home primarily through Crane's efforts. Among the best of the fairy tales were *Beauty and the Beast* and *The Frog Prince*, both published in 1874, and *The Yellow Dwarf* and *Jack and the Beanstalk*, which Crane designed a year later.

Among Crane's finest and most successful works were his primers and his alphabet books. The latter proved to be so popular that Crane created no less than six titles of very different character for Routledge's "Sixpenny Toy Series" between 1865 (*The Railroad Alphabet* and *The Farmyard Alphabet*) and 1875 (*Baby's Own Alphabet*). In 1872 *Noah's Ark Alphabet* was published; but the two best books, from an artistic point of view, were published one after the other in 1874, a time when Crane was at the very top of his form. These were *The Absurd ABC* and *An Alphabet of Old Friends*, both of which speak eloquently for themselves in the reproductions that follow. In a great number of families, it was *The Absurd ABC* (sometimes referred to as *The Absurd Alphabet*) that first exposed young readers to Crane's genius. There could be no nicer way of learning one's ABCs than through either of these books – and children adored them both. I doubt that any finer children's alphabets have ever been designed.

In documenting the early "Toy Books," confusion frequently arises not only from the fact that these paperbacks were continually being reprinted without mention of the date, but also because frequently they were reissued in a different form. In 1871, for instance, Routledge, hitting on a plan that would enable them to take even fuller advantage of these highly remunerative properties, started packaging several of the "Toy Books" together in single "gift" volumes. Each was given a new title page, new endpapers, and a cloth binding. One of the nicest in this category was *The Goody Two Shoes' Picture Book*. This collection of Crane's classics comprised "Goody Two Shoes," "The Frog Prince," "Beauty and the Beast," as well as "An Alphabet of Old Friends," from which the reproductions in the first part of the present volume were made

According to records, after 1874, no further collections appeared until 1895 when the idea was revived by a different publisher – John Lane, The Bodley Head – who made arrangements to publish a four-volume *Walter Crane's Picture Book* using the old Edmund Evans color blocks. It was John Lane who reissued the edition of *The Absurd ABC* from which the second part of this volume has been reproduced.

In the decade beginning 1875, Crane continued to illustrate an average of three books a year, as he had done earlier. Not all of these were of the "Toy Book" type, and some titles were for adult readers. Among his many noted successes after 1875 were: *The Baby's Opera, A Book of Old Rhymes with New Dresses* (1877), *Household Stories from the Collection of the Brothers Grimm* (1882), *The Happy Prince And Other Tales* by Oscar Wilde (1888), *A Wonder Book for Girls and Boys* by Nathaniel Hawthorne (1892), *The Merry Wives of Windsor* by William Shakespeare (1894), and *Flowers from Shakespeare's Garden; a Posy from the Plays* (1906).

When he first started designing books for children Crane had no children of his own, but after marrying Mary Frances Andrews in 1871 he was to have three, Beatrice, Lionel, and Lancelot. Meanwhile, as he was establishing himself in the 1860s, he made a point of studying the Victorian child's attitude toward books in general and toward his own in particular.

"Like the ancient Egyptians," Crane once said, "children appear to see most things in profile and like definite statement in design. They prefer well-defined forms and bright frank colour. They don't want to bother about three dimensions."

On another occasion Crane observed, "The best of designing for children is that the imagination and fancy may be let loose and roam freely, and there is always room for humour and even pathos, sure of being followed by that ever-living sense of wonder and romance in the child heart – a heart which in some cases, happily, never grows up or grows old." It would seem that Walter Crane's never did.

Bryan Holme

AN ALPHABET OF OLD FRIENDS.

A
A carrion crow sat on an oak,
Watching a tailor shape his cloak.
"Wife, bring me my old bent bow,
That I may shoot yon carrion crow."
The tailor he shot and missed his mark,
And shot his own sow quite through the heart.
"Wife, wife, bring brandy in a spoon,
For our old sow is in a swoon."

B
Ba, ba, black sheep,
   Have you any wool?
Yes, marry, have I,
   Three bags full.

One for my master,
   One for my dame,
But none for the little boy
   That cries in the lane.

C
Hen. Cock, cock, I have la-a-ayed!
Cock. Hen, hen, that's well sa-a-ayed!
Hen. Although I have to go bare-footed every day-a-ay!
Cock. (*Con spirito.*) Sell your eggs and buy shoes!
                   Sell your eggs and buy shoes!

D
Dickery, dickery, dock,
The mouse ran up the clock.
   The clock struck one,
   Down the mouse ran,
Dickery, dickery, dock.

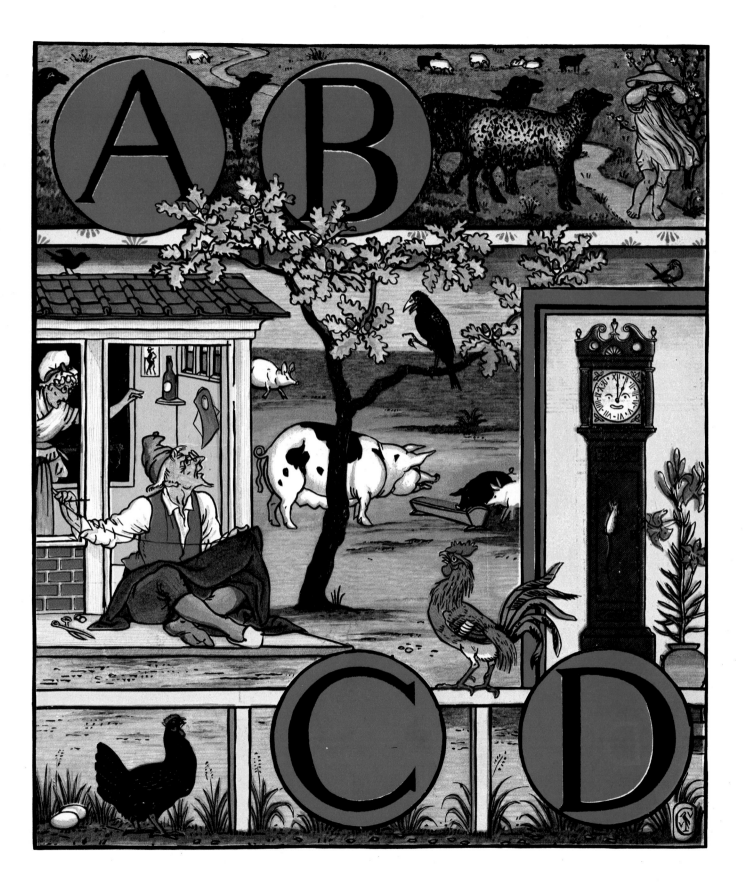

An Alphabet of Old Friends.

E Elizabeth, Elspeth, Betsy, and Bess,
They all went together to seek a bird's nest
They found a bird's nest with five eggs in;
They all took one, and left four in.

F Father, father, I've come to confess.
O, yes, dear daughter, what have you done?

G Gang and hear the owl yell,
Sit and see the swallow flee,
See the foal before its mither's e'e,
'Twill be a thriving year wi' thee.

H Hush-a-bye, baby, on the tree-top;
When the wind blows the cradle will rock;
When the wind ceases the cradle will fall,
And down will come baby and cradle and all.

An Alphabet of Old Friends.

I had a little husband
   No bigger than my thumb;
I put him in a pint pot,
   And there I bade him drum.
I bought a little horse
   That galloped up and down;
I bridled him, and saddled him,
   And sent him out of town.
I gave him a pair of garters,
   To tie up his little hose,
And a little silk handkerchief,
   To wipe his little nose.

J   Jack Sprat would eat no fat,
His wife would eat no lean;
Was not that a pretty trick
To make the platter clean?

K King Cole was a merry old soul,
   And a merry old soul was he.
He called for his pipe, and he called for his bowl,
   And he called for his fiddlers three
   Every fiddler had a fiddle,
   And a very fine fiddle had he:
Twee, tweedle dee, tweedle dee, went the fiddlers.
   Oh, there's none so rare
   As can compare
With King Cole and his fiddlers three!

An Alphabet of Old Friends.

L

Little Bo-peep has lost her sheep,
    And can't tell where to find them.
Let them alone and they'll come home,
    And bring their tails behind them, &c.

M

Mistress Mary,
    Quite contrary,
How does your garden grow?
    With silver bells,
    And cockle shells.
And cowslips all of a-row.

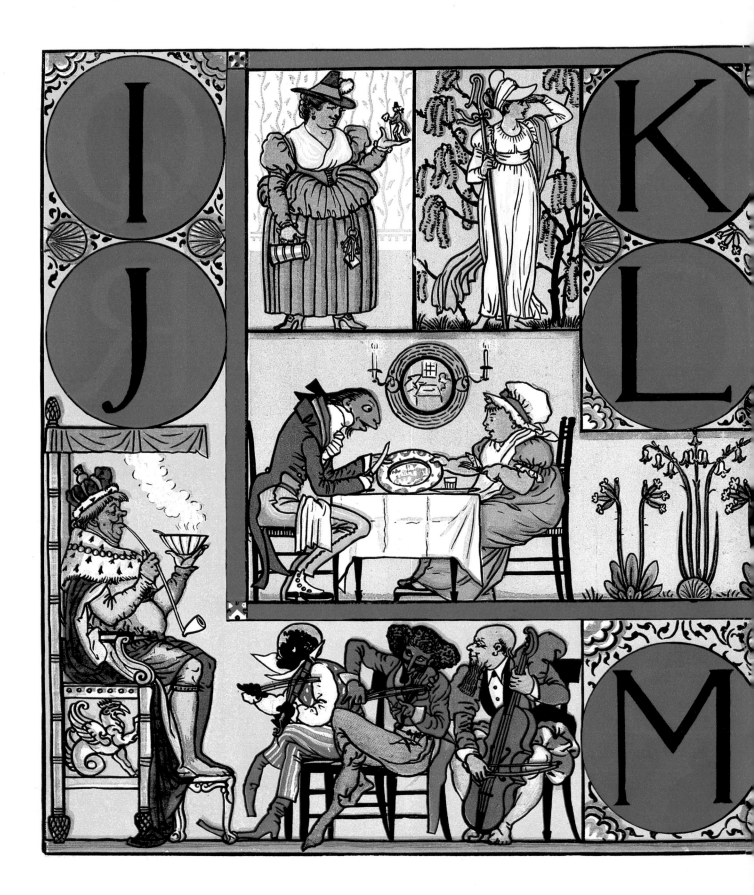

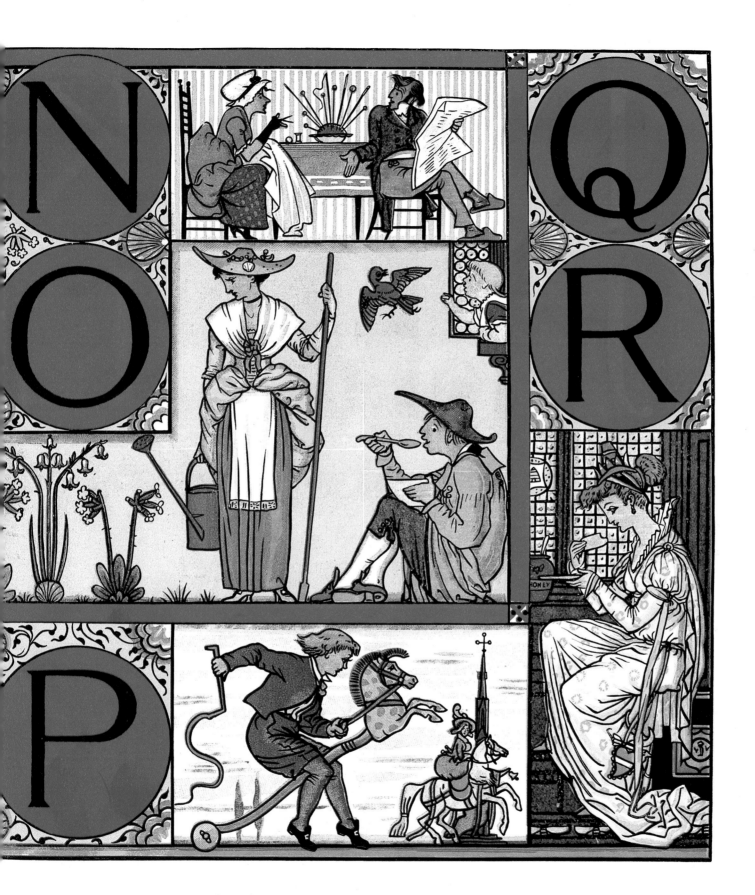

An Alphabet of Old Friends.

N Needles and pins, needles and pins,
When a man marries his trouble begins.

O Once I saw a little bird,
  Come hop, hop, hop;
So I cried, " Little bird,
  Will you stop, stop, stop?"
And was going to the window,
  To say, " How do you do?"
When he shook his little tail,
  And far away he flew.

P Pease-pudding hot, pease-pudding cold;
Pease-pudding in the pot, nine days old.

Q Queen was in the parlour, eating bread and honey.

R Ride a-cock horse to Banbury Cross,
To see an old woman get up on her horse;
Rings on her fingers and bells at her toes,
And so she makes music wherever she goes.

An Alphabet of Old Friends.

S
Simple Simon met a pieman,
  Going to the fair;
Says Simple Simon to the pieman,
  " Let me taste your ware!"

T
Taffy was a Welshman,
  Taffy was a thief,
Taffy came to my house,
  And stole a leg of beef.

I went to Taffy's house,
  Taffy was not at home;

Taffy came to my house,
  And stole a marrow-bone.

I went to Taffy's house,
  Taffy was in bed;
I took the marrow-bone,
  And broke Taffy's head.

An Alphabet of Old Friends.

U

Up hill and down dale,
Butter is made in every vale;
And if Nancy Cock
Is a good girl,
She shall have a spouse,
And make butter anon,
Before her old grandmother
Grows a young man.

V

Valentine, Oh, Valentine,
  Curl your locks as I do mine;
Two before and two behind;
  Good-morrow to you, Valentine.

W

" Where are you going, my pretty maid ? "
" I'm going a milking, sir," she said.
" May I go with you, my pretty maid ? "
" You're kindly welcome, sir," she said.
" What is your father, my pretty maid ? "
" My father's a farmer, sir," she said.
" Say will you marry me, my pretty maid ? "
" Yes, if you please, kind sir," she said.
" What is your fortune, my pretty maid ? "
" My face is my fortune, sir," she said.
" Then, I won't marry you, my pretty maid ! "
" Nobody asked you, sir," she said.

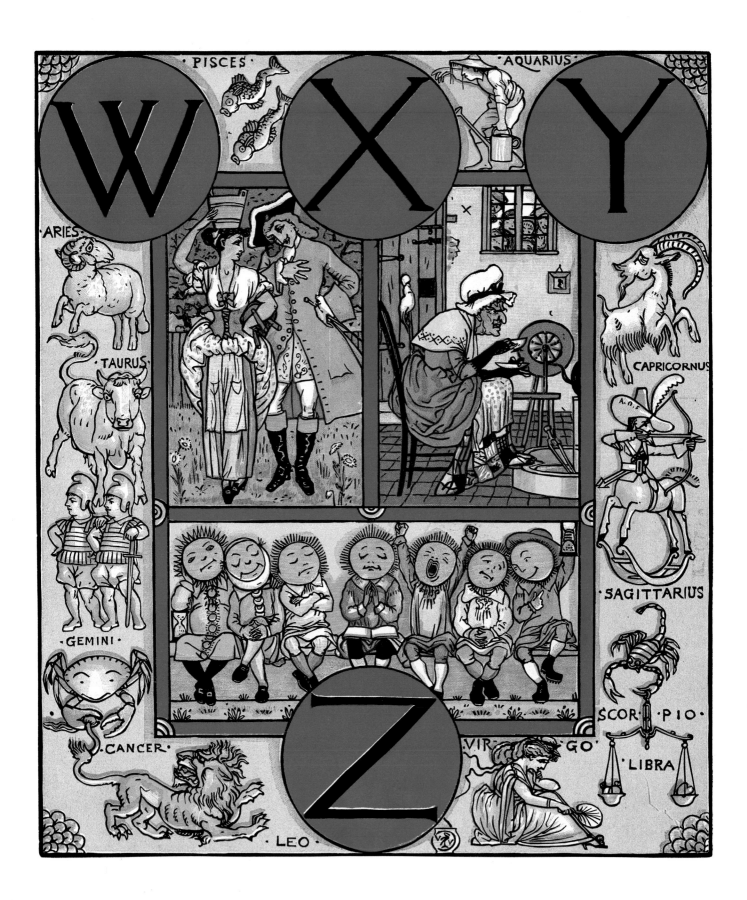

An Alphabet of Old Friends.

X Cross **X** patch,
Draw the latch,
Sit by the fire and spin :

Take a cup
And drink it up,
Then call the neighbours in.

Y You know that Monday is Sunday's brother ;
Tuesday is such another ;
Wednesday you must go to church and pray ;
Thursday is half-holiday ;
On Friday it is too late to begin to spin,
And Saturday is half-holiday again.

Z ZODIAC FOR THE NURSERY.
The ram, the bull, the heavenly twins,
And next the crab, the lion shines,
The virgin and the scales,
The scorpion, archer, and the goat,
The man who holds the watering-pot,
And fish with glittering scales.

·WALTER·CRANE'S·
·PICTURE·BOOKS·
·RE·ISSUE·

·THE· ·ABSURD· ·A·B·C

·JOHN·LANE·
·THE·BODLEY·HEAD·
·LONDON·&·NEW·
·YORK·

A for the APPLE or Alphabet pie, Which all get a slice of. Come taste it & try.

EFGHIJKLMNO

C for the CAT that played on the fiddle, When cows jumped higher than Heigh Diddle, Diddle!

D for the DAME with her pig at the stile, 'Tis said they got over, but not yet a while.

B is the BABY who gave Mr Bunting Full many a long days rabbit skin hunting.

E F G

E for the Englishman,
ready to make fast
The giant who wanted to
have him for breakfast.

F for the Frog in the story
you know,
Begun with a wooing but
ending in woe.

G for Goosey Gander
who wandered upstairs,
And met the old man
who objected to prayers.

H for poor Humpty who after his fall.
Felt obliged to resign his seat on the wall.

I for the Inn where they wouldn't give beer,
To one with too much and no money, I fear.

J does for poor Jack and also for Jill,
Who had so disastrous a tumble down hill.

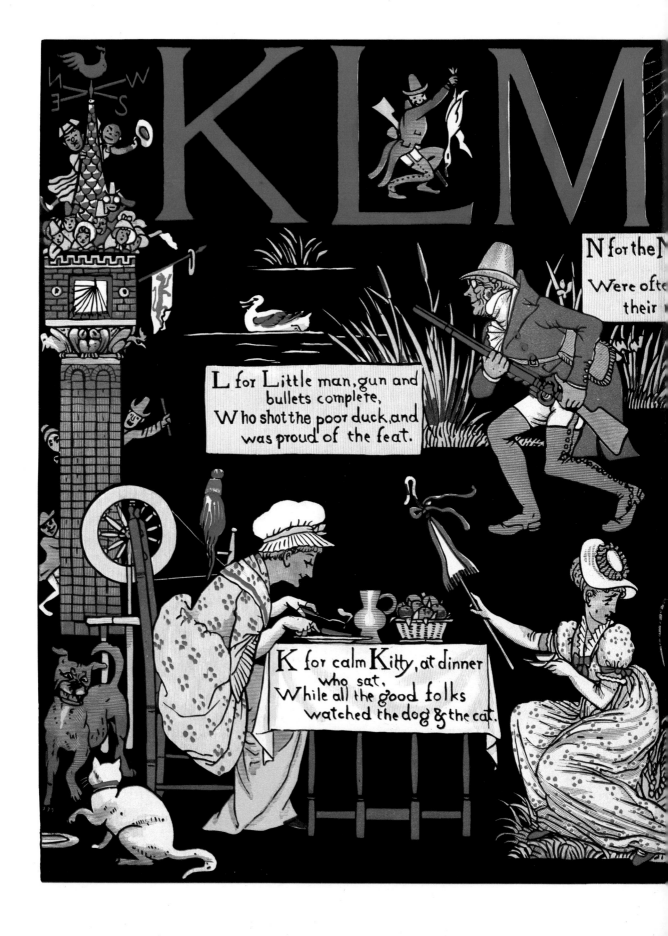

KLM

L for Little man, gun and bullets complete, Who shot the poor duck, and was proud of the feat.

K for calm Kitty, at dinner who sat, While all the good folks watched the dog & the cat.

NOPQ

...erous children,
...who
...o much for
...her in Shoe

O the Old person that
cobwebs did spy,
And went up to sweep e'm
Oh ever so high !

M for Miss Muffet, with
that horrid spider,
Just dropped into tea and
a chat beside her.

P for the Pie made of
blackbirds to sing,
A song fit for supper
a dish for a king.

Q for Queen Anne
who sat in the sun
Till she, more than the lily
resembled the bun

R stands for Richard &
Robert, those men
Who didn't get up one
fine morning till ten!

S for the Snail that showed
wonderful fight,
Putting no less than twenty
four tailors to flight?

T stands for Tom, the son of the piper,
May his principles change as his years grow riper.

U for the Unicorn, keeping his eye on
The coveted crown, and 'ts counsel the Lion.

V for the Victuals, including the drink,
The old woman lived on surprising to think!